Daily

Evening

Devotions

—.—

Biblical Teachings

CONTENTS

FOREWORD

Welcome to the second half of our devotional series for teen boys! If you're new here, we highly recommend checking out the first half of the series, *Daily Morning Devotional for Teen Boys: 5-Minute Devotions To Win Your Day Driven By Purpose, Faith, And Confidence.*, to get the full picture.

In this book, we focus on evening devotionals to help you wind down after a long day and to reflect on the events of the day with the guidance of scripture.

INTRODUCTION

I know what it's like to be a teenage boy growing up in a modern world. It wasn't too long ago that I was in your shoes. I remember the struggles of growing up - continuously experiencing new events, adventures, types of people/personalities, emotions, and more. It gets overwhelming, and in many cases, you might not know how to react or how you should feel. My goal with this devotional book is to offer a guide to teen boys, such as yourself, who might need some grounding. Remember, life is confusing, and you're not meant to have it all figured out. Enjoy the ups and the downs because one day, you will look back and be proud of yourself for getting through it all and out the other side.

I personally think now is a more challenging time than ever to grow up. There are vast distractions in the modern world set out to divert your attention from your true goals in life and slow down your growth as a young man. Social media, TikTok, 18+ material, etc. are all going to shape your brain to believe what isn't true. What you see on these platforms is highly edited and made out to be much greater than it really is. It might sound hard to believe for you now, but through God, you will thrive as a young man instead of filling your brain with toxicity and fake realities.

Your teenage years are the most life-defining. Infinite amounts of progress can be made here to shape your character, should you decide to work on yourself, and your faith. Most teenagers won't take advantage of this time and will be easily led astray due to peer pressure and social acceptance. However, you can use it to your own advantage to become a cut above the rest and the best man you can be. You can use these devotionals to help start using your time wisely and grow yourself as a young man. This might sound overwhelming but fear not; God is, and always will be, on your side and will offer you the utmost guidance and security to achieve the goals you set for yourself.

Only 5 minutes each evening reading through these daily devotionals will allow you to embrace the Lord before you rest for the night. You can even do it while sitting in bed. That's how easy it is! There's no rush to finish the book, so you shouldn't worry if you miss the odd evening. God loves you and will never abandon you.

SUGGESTIONS ON HOW TO USE THIS BOOK

The devotions are designed to be read each evening before you end your day. That way, you can reflect on how the Lord has been present in your day, in your decisions and actions, and prepare yourself for the next day ahead. You can read them before or after dinner, before bedtime, or any other time that works for you. By spending time with the Lord each evening, you can find peace and rest in His presence, and set your heart and mind on God before you sleep. Plan a time when you will read, and try to keep that plan as best as you can. As I've said, don't worry if there are times when you miss an evening. Life happens.

Date the page and read the scripture verse. Take a minute to let the words sink in. Reread the verse. Then read the devotion that goes with the text. If you have time, you can read the "rest of the story" if there's a reference given. Next, read the questions and think about your answers. Finish up with the prayer, and you're done for the day! If you like to write, having a separate journal is a good idea. If you don't like to write, that's okay, too. Just be sure and spend time thinking about your answers to the questions asked. That's how God will speak directly to *you* and tell *you* what God wanted *you* to learn that day.

Each of the verses tell you where to look for them; verses and chapters are pretty standard, no matter the translation of the bible you have. It can add to your understanding by reading different translations if the ones in this book are slightly different to your bible. Compare the two and see if that changes the meaning in any way.

If you happen to have a friend or family member who is interested in doing these devotions with you, that would be a good way to read and work together. You could talk about the questions and learn from each other. If not, you are fine working on your own, because you really aren't doing it alone. The Holy Spirit is with you to guide your understanding, always.

May God bless and keep you, may God 's face shine upon you, may God give you peace and understanding.

Amen.

1
— · —

REFLECTION

___/___/_____

"Examine yourselves to see whether you are in the faith; test yourselves."

- 2 CORINTHIANS 13:5

In the busyness of life, it's easy to get caught up in our own thoughts and feelings. But taking time to reflect on our actions, thoughts, and motivations can help us grow in self-awareness, make better choices, and deepen our relationship with God.

Spend time reflecting on the day's events and how they align with your values and faith.

Reflection:

How can you make time for reflection and self-examination in your busy life?

Prayer:

Dear God,

Help me to make time for reflection and self-examination in my daily life. Give me the courage to face my shortcomings and to seek your guidance and wisdom. Help me to grow in self-awareness and to become the person you created me to be.

Amen.

2

TRUSTING GOD

___/___/_____

"Trust in the Lord with all your heart and lean not on your own under-standing; in all your ways submit to him, and he will make your paths straight."

- PROVERBS 3:5-6

S ometimes life can be overwhelming, and we may not know what to do. But God promises to guide us if we trust Him. For example, imagine you have an important exam coming up, and you feel like you haven't studied enough. Instead of panicking, you can trust that God will help you remember what you need to know and give you the wisdom to answer the questions.

Reflection:

Do you trust God to put you on the right path? He will as long as you put the work in too.

How can you deepen your trust in God and rely on his promises?

Prayer:

Dear God,

Help me to trust in your goodness and faithfulness, even when life is hard. Give me the courage to step out in faith and to trust that you will provide for my needs. Help me to remember your promises and to trust in your unfailing love.

Amen.

3

_ . _

OBEDIENCE

___/___/_____

"If you love me, keep my commands."

It can be easy to think that we know what's best for ourselves, but God's ways are higher than ours. We show our love for Him by obeying His commands, even when we don't fully understand them. For example, maybe your friends are pressuring you to do something that goes against what you believe is right. Instead of giving in, you can obey God and stand firm in your convictions.

Reflection:

Do you consider yourself to be an obedient person?

In what areas of your life do you struggle with obedience to God's commands?

Prayer:

Dear God,

Help me to be obedient to your commands and to follow your will for my life. Give me the strength to resist temptation and to choose obedience over sin. Help me to trust in your plan for my life, even when it is difficult.

Amen.

4

FAITH

___/___/_____

"Now faith is confidence in what we hope for and assurance about what we do not see."

- HEBREWS 11:1

F aith means believing in something we can't see. We can have faith in God's promises even if we can't physically see them. For example, maybe you're going through a tough time, and it seems like God is distant. You can have faith that He is still with you and that He has a plan for your life, even if you can't see it yet.

Reflection:

Do you have faith that God will help you through tough times?

How can you strengthen your faith in God?

Prayer:

Dear God,

Help me to grow in my faith and trust in you more each day. Help me to lean on you in times of doubt and uncertainty, and to remember that with you, all things are possible. Strengthen my faith and give me the courage to follow where you lead. Amen.

5

— · —

Prayer

___/___/_____

"Do not be anxious about anything, but in every situation, by prayer and petition, with thanksgiving, present your requests to God."

- Philippians 4:6

P rayer is simply talking to God. We can bring our worries, fears, and joys to Him and trust that He hears us. For example, maybe you're struggling with a particular sin and you don't know how to overcome it. Instead of trying to handle it on your own, you can pray and ask God to give you strength and wisdom to resist temptation.

Reflection:

How often do you pray?

How can you deepen your prayer life and grow closer to God?

Prayer:

Dear God,

Help me to prioritize prayer in my daily life. Teach me to listen to your voice and seek your will through prayer. Strengthen my faith and draw me closer to you as I seek to know you more through prayer.

Amen.

6

—·—

SERVICE

___/___/_____

*"Each of you should use whatever gift you have received to serve others as
faithful stewards of God's grace in its various forms."*

- I PETER 4:10

J esus set an example for us by serving others, and we can follow in His
footsteps by using our gifts and talents to help those around us. For
example, maybe you're good at sports, so you could volunteer to coach a
younger team. Or maybe you're good at playing music, so you could use
your talent to lead worship at church.

Reflection:

In what ways can you serve others and make a difference in the world?

Prayer:

Dear God,

Thank you for the opportunity to serve others. Help me to be humble and selfless, and to use my talents and resources to help those in need. Give me a heart of compassion and a desire to make a positive impact in the world.

Amen.

7

— . —

FORGIVENESS

___/___/_____

"Bear with each other and forgive one another if any of you has a grievance against someone. Forgive as the Lord forgave you."

- COLOSSIANS 3:13

J esus forgave us of our sins, and we are called to forgive others as well. Forgiveness doesn't mean that we excuse someone's wrongdoing, but it means that we let go of any anger or bitterness toward them. For example, maybe someone has hurt you in the past and it's been hard to forgive them. Instead of holding onto that hurt, you can choose to forgive them and ask God to help you heal.

Reflection:

Is there anyone you struggle to forgive?

How can you practice forgiveness in your daily life?

Prayer:

Dear God,

Help me to forgive those who have wronged me, just as you have forgiven me. Give me the strength to let go of anger and bitterness, and help me to show others the same grace that you have shown me.

Amen,

8

— . —

HUMILITY

___/___/_____

"Do nothing out of selfish ambition or vain conceit. Rather, in humility value others above yourselves, not looking to your own interests but each of you to the interests of the others."

- PHILIPPIANS 2:3-4

H umility means putting others before ourselves and recognizing that we are not the center of the universe. We can show humility by serving others and not seeking attention or praise for ourselves. For example, maybe you're good at a particular skill, and you're tempted to show off or brag about it. Instead, you can choose to use that skill to serve others and point the focus back to God.

Reflection:

Think back to a time when you've shown humility. What happened?

How can you develop a humble spirit and put others first?

Prayer:

Dear God,

Please help me to have a humble spirit and to put the needs of others before my own. Teach me to serve others as you have served us.

Amen.

9

PURITY

___/___/_____

"Blessed are the pure in heart, for they will see God."

- MATTHEW 5:8 (NIV)

P urity is about living a life that is pleasing to God and avoiding things that can lead us astray from His path. This includes being mindful of the media we consume, the people we surround ourselves with, and the choices we make in our daily lives. By striving for purity, we can cultivate a heart and mind that is focused on God and His will for our lives. It's not always easy, but through prayer, self-discipline, and a reliance on God's grace, we can stay on the path of purity.

In a world that often celebrates impurity, it takes courage and strength to choose to live a life of purity. But by choosing to guard your heart and mind, you set yourself apart for a greater purpose and for deeper intimacy with God.

Reflection:

How can you maintain purity in your thoughts and actions?

Prayer:

Dear God,

Help me to keep my thoughts and actions pure. Give me the strength to resist temptation and to always follow your ways.

Amen.

10

COURAGE

___/___/_____

"Have I not commanded you? Be strong and courageous. Do not be afraid;
do not be discouraged, for the Lord your God will be with you wherever you
go. "

- JOSHUA 1:9

F ear can hold us back from doing what God has called us to do, but He promises to be with us always. We can be courageous in the face of fear by trusting in God's strength and not our own. For example, maybe you're afraid to share your faith with someone because you're worried about how they'll react. Instead of giving in to fear, you can choose to be courageous and trust that God will give you the words to say and the strength to speak up. Or maybe you're facing a difficult situation at school or at home, and you're not sure how to handle it. Instead of giving in to fear, you can choose to be courageous and trust that God is with you every step of the way.

Reflection:

Take a moment to think about some moments where you've shown courage.

What steps can you take to develop courage and stand up for what is right?

Prayer:

Dear God,

Give me the courage to stand up for what is right and to be a voice for those who cannot speak for themselves. Help me to trust in you and not be afraid.

Amen.

11

— · —

LOVE

___/___/_____

"Above all, love each other deeply because love covers over a multitude of sins."

- I PETER 4:8

Love is the greatest commandment, and it's what Jesus exemplified throughout His life. We can love others by showing them kindness, compassion, and forgiveness. For example, maybe someone has hurt you or wronged you in some way, and it's hard to love them. Instead of holding onto bitterness or anger, you can choose to love them by praying for them, forgiving them, and treating them with kindness and respect. Or maybe you see someone who is hurting or in need, and you can choose to love them by offering a listening ear, a helping hand, or a kind word.

Reflection:

Are you a loving person? Who do you show your love to? Who/what do you love? How do you show love? How can you show love to those around you, even when it's difficult?

Prayer:

Dear God,

Please fill me with your love so that I can show love to those around me, even when it's hard. Help me to love others as you have loved me.

Amen.

12

— · —

IDENTITY

___/___/_____

"Therefore, if anyone is in Christ, the new creation has come: The old has gone, the new is here!"

- 2 CORINTHIANS 5:17

As a teenager, it can be easy to get caught up in the opinions of others and to base your identity on what they think of you. But your true identity is found in Christ, and He has created you with a purpose and a plan. Think about what you're passionate about and what makes you unique, and use those things to glorify God. Remember that you are a new creation in Christ and that your old self has passed away.

Reflection:

How can you find your identity in Christ and not in what the world says about you?

Prayer:

Dear God,

Help me to find my identity in you and not in the things of this world. Show me who you created me to be and help me to live out that purpose.

Amen.

13

— · —

PERSEVERANCE

___/___/_____

"Let perseverance finish its work so that you may be mature and complete, not lacking anything."

- JAMES 1:4

L ife can be tough, and you may face obstacles that seem impossible to overcome. But don't give up! God is with you, and He promises to give you the strength to endure. Keep pushing forward, and don't be afraid to ask for help when you need it. You are capable of more than you realize, and with God's help, you can overcome any challenge.

Reflection:

Are you someone who perseveres at a task until you reach your goal?

How can you develop a mindset of perseverance in the face of challenges?

Prayer:

Dear God,

Help me to be strong and persevere through challenges. Help me to remember that with your help, I can overcome any obstacle.

Amen.

14

TEMPTATION

___/___/_____

"No temptation has overtaken you except what is common to mankind.
And God is faithful; he will not let you be tempted beyond what you can
bear. But when you are tempted, he will also provide a way out so that you
can endure it."

- I CORINTHIANS 10:13

We all face temptation at one point or another, and it can be hard to resist. But remember that God will never tempt you beyond what you can bear and will always provide a way out. Stay strong in your faith, and surround yourself with people who will encourage and support you. And when you do stumble, remember that God is always ready to forgive and restore you.

Reflection:

Take some time to think of all the things that tempt you. Why do they tempt you?

What steps can you take to resist temptation and stay on the right path?

Prayer:

Dear God,

Please give me the strength to resist temptation and to always follow your path. Help me to remember that with your help, I can overcome any temptation.

Amen.

15

—·—

FRIENDSHIP

___/___/_____

"A friend loves at all times, and a brother is born in a time of adversity."

- PROVERBS 17:17

G ood friends are a blessing, and they can help us grow in our faith, stay accountable, and be there for us in tough times. But not all friends are created equal, so it's important to choose wisely. Seek out friends who will encourage you in your faith and hold you accountable when you need it. And don't be afraid to be that kind of friend to others as well.

Reflection:

What do you think makes someone a good friend? Who are your *true* friends?

How can you be a better friend to those around you?

Prayer:

Dear God,

Help me to be a good friend to those around me. Give me the wisdom to know how to encourage and support them in their times of need.

Amen.

16

— · —

GRATITUDE

___/___/_____

"Give thanks in all circumstances; for this is God's will for you in Christ Jesus."

- I THESSALONIANS 5:18

It's easy to focus on what we don't have or what's going wrong in our lives, but God calls us to be thankful in all circumstances. Take time each day to reflect on the blessings in your life, no matter how small they may seem. And when things are tough, remember that God is with you and will never leave you.

Reflection:

Reflect and take some time to think of all the things you're grateful for - matter how small or big they might be.

What are some practical ways you can cultivate a heart of gratitude?

Prayer:

Dear God,

Thank you for all the blessings you have given me. Help me to have a grateful heart and to never take your blessings for granted.

Amen.

17

— · —

HOPE

___/___/_____

"May the God of hope fill you with all joy and peace as you trust in him, so that you may overflow with hope by the power of the Holy Spirit."

- ROMANS 15:13

Hope is a powerful force that can sustain us through even the darkest times. Remember that as a Christian, you have a hope that goes beyond this life and extends into eternity. Keep your eyes fixed on God and His promises, and don't be afraid to share that hope with others who may be struggling.

Reflection:

What gives you hope, even in difficult times?

Prayer:

Dear God,

Please fill me with hope, even when things seem dark and uncertain. Help me to trust in your goodness and to hold onto the hope that comes from knowing you.

Amen.

18

Purpose

___/___/_____

"For we are God's handiwork, created in Christ Jesus to do good works, which God prepared in advance for us to do."

As a teenager, it can be easy to feel lost or uncertain about your purpose in life. But remember that God has created you with a specific purpose and has given you unique gifts and talents to fulfill it. Seek His guidance and direction, and don't be afraid to step out in faith and pursue your passions.

Reflection:

Do you have a purpose in life? If not, that's okay - it takes time to find it.

What are you currently doing to seek out your purpose in your daily life?

Prayer:

Dear God,

Please help me to discern my purpose and to live a life that is meaningful and fulfilling. Give me the courage to pursue my passions and the humility to seek guidance and wisdom from others.

Amen.

19

—.—

STEWARDSHIP

___/___/_____

"Moreover, it is required of stewards that they be found faithful."

- I CORINTHIANS 4:2

God has entrusted us with many gifts and blessings, and we are called to be good stewards of them. Use your resources wisely and generously to bless others and advance God's kingdom. Remember that everything you have ultimately belongs to God, and He will reward those who are faithful with what He has given them.

Reflection:

What does it mean to be a good steward of the resources and talents God has given you?

Prayer:

Dear God,

Please help me to use my talents and resources in a way that honors you and benefits others. Give me the wisdom to manage my time and resources well, and the generosity to share with those in need. Amen.

20

—˙—

COURAGEOUS LEADERSHIP

___/___/_____

"Have I not commanded you? Be strong and courageous. Do not be afraid; do not be discouraged, for the Lord your God will be with you wherever you go."

- JOSHUA 1:9

As a teenager, you have the opportunity to be a leader and influencer in your world. But that requires courage and conviction to stand up for what is right and speak out against injustice. Don't be afraid to take a stand, even when it's unpopular or difficult. Remember that God is with you and will use your leadership for His glory.

Reflection:

What does it mean to be a courageous leader, and what are some ways you can practice this in your daily life?

Can you think of a time you've been a courageous leader?

Prayer:

Dear God,

Please help me to be a leader who inspires others and leads with courage and compassion. Give me the wisdom to make good decisions and the courage to stand up for what is right. Amen.

21

—·—

REST

___/___/_____

"We can find rest in God and His promises, and we should prioritize rest in our lives to avoid burnout and fatigue. "Come to me, all you who are weary and burdened, and I will give you rest. Take my yoke upon you and learn from me, for I am gentle and humble in heart, and you will find rest for your souls."

- MATTHEW 11:28-29

As a teen, it's easy to feel like you need to be constantly busy and productive. But God knows the value of rest, and He wants us to take time to recharge. In Matthew 11:28-29, Jesus invites us to come to Him when we are tired and burdened, and He promises to give us rest. Take time to disconnect from your daily routine and enjoy the peace that comes from spending time with God. Remember that true rest and renewal come from Him.

Reflection:

Are you taking enough time to make sure you have proper rest and time to recharge?

In what ways do you struggle to rest and take care of yourself?

Prayer:

Dear God,

Please help me to rest in your love and to take care of my body and mind. Give me the strength to say no to things that drain me, and the courage to prioritize rest and self-care.

Amen.

22

WISDOM

___/___/_____

"For the Lord gives wisdom; from his mouth comes knowledge and under-standing."

- PROVERBS 2:6

A s a teenager, it's normal to feel lost or unsure of what to do. But know that seeking wisdom is always a good choice. Turn to trusted adults, mentors, and spiritual leaders for guidance, and most importantly, pray for wisdom and direction. Remember that God is always there to provide wisdom when you ask for it, so never hesitate to seek his guidance.

Reflection:

What does wisdom mean to you, and how do you seek to grow in wisdom?

Do you know anyone who is wise?

Prayer:

Dear God,

Please give me the wisdom to make good decisions and to discern what is right and true. Help me to seek wisdom from you and from those who are wiser than me.

Amen.

23

— · —

OBEDIENCE

___/___/_____

"But be doers of the word, and not hearers only, deceiving yourselves."

- JAMES 1:22

O bedience can sometimes seem like a daunting task, but it's an important aspect of a healthy and faithful life. Start by being obedient to your parents and other authority figures in your life. This means following rules and guidelines, even if you don't always agree with them. Additionally, seek to live out your faith in your actions, treating others with love and respect, and striving to follow Jesus' example. Remember that obedience is a journey, so don't be discouraged if you stumble along the way.

Reflection:

Are you good at following the rules? Are there any rules you don't like to follow? Why?

What are some areas of your life where you struggle to be obedient?

Prayer:

Dear God,

Please help me to follow your commands and to do what is right even when it is hard. Give me the strength to resist temptation and to live a life that is pleasing to you.

Amen.

24

— . —

EVANGELISM

___/___/_____

"Therefore go and make disciples of all nations, baptizing them in the name of the Father and of the Son and of the Holy Spirit."

- MATTHEW 28:19

S haring your faith with others can be intimidating, but it's an essential part of being a follower of Christ. Start by living out your faith in your everyday interactions with others, showing kindness and love to everyone you encounter. Look for opportunities to share your faith, but also know that sometimes your actions will speak louder than your words. Above all, trust in God to guide you as you seek to share the good news of his love with those around you.

Reflection:

What does evangelism mean to you, and why is it important?

How can you share your faith with others?

Prayer:

Dear God,

Please give me the courage to share your love and truth with those around me. Help me to be a light in the darkness and to spread your message of hope to those who need it most.

Amen.

25

PATIENCE

___/___/_____

"And let us not grow weary while doing good, for in due season we shall reap if we do not lose heart."

- GALATIANS 6:9

A teenage boy who loves playing basketball was having trouble with his jump shot. He became frustrated and angry because he had practiced for a while but still couldn't get it right. His coach told him that learning a new skill takes time and patience, and encouraged him to keep practicing. The teenager didn't give up and continued to work hard, even when it was tough. After weeks of dedication, he finally hit his first three-pointer. The boy learned that being patient and persistent pays off in the end.

Reflection:

Are you a patient person?

In what areas of your life do you struggle with being patient?

Prayer:

Dear God,

Please help me to be patient with myself and with others. When I feel frustrated or discouraged, remind me to take a deep breath and trust that things will work out in the end.

Amen.

26

—·—

TRUST

___/___/_____

"Trust in the Lord with all your heart and lean not on your own understanding; in all your ways submit to him, and he will make your paths straight."

- PROVERBS 3:5-6

T rusting in God is not always easy, especially when we face uncertainty and challenges in life. But the Bible encourages us to trust in the Lord with all our hearts, to submit to Him, and to follow His ways. We may not always understand God's plan, but we can trust that He has our best interests at heart and will guide us on the right path. Teens should learn to trust God in all areas of their lives, whether it's their future plans, relationships, or personal struggles. Spend time in prayer, seek His guidance, and trust in His plan.

Reflection:

Do you give your trust to the Lord?

What are some ways that you struggle with trusting others or with trusting God?

Prayer:

Dear God,

Please help me to trust in your plans for my life and to trust the people around me. Give me the courage to be vulnerable and open with others, and to trust that they will treat me with kindness and respect.

Amen.

27

— . —

CONTENTMENT

___/___/_____

"I have learned to be content whatever the circumstances. I know what it is to be in need, and I know what it is to have plenty. I have learned the secret of being content in any and every situation, whether well fed or hungry, whether living in plenty or in want."

- PHILIPPIANS 4:11-12

A teenage boy was always comparing himself to his friends on social media. He felt like he didn't measure up and was never satisfied with what he had. One day, he read a Bible verse about being content with what you have and not coveting what others possess. He decided to change his mindset and focus on being grateful for the blessings in his life, instead of constantly wanting more. Over time, he learned that true happiness comes from within and not from material possessions.

Reflection:

What are some ways you can cultivate a sense of contentment and gratitude in your life?

Prayer:

Dear God,

Help me to find contentment and joy in all circumstances. Give me the gratitude to appreciate the blessings in my life and the peace that comes from trusting in you.

Amen.

28

— . —

COMPASSION

___/___/_____

"Therefore, as God's chosen people, holy and dearly loved, clothe yourselves with compassion, kindness, humility, gentleness, and patience."

— COLOSSIANS 3:12

A teenage boy witnessed a classmate being bullied by a group of students. He felt empathy for the student and knew he had to do something. He approached the student and offered his friendship and support. He also reported the bullying to the school authorities. Over time, the bullied student felt more accepted and included, and the teenager felt good about standing up for what was right.

Reflection:

When was the last time you showed compassion? What happened?

How can you show more compassion and kindness to others?

Prayer:

Dear God,

Help me to be a compassionate and kind person. Give me the empathy to understand the needs of others and the willingness to help them in any way I can.

Amen.

29

— · —

INTEGRITY

___/___/_____

"The righteous person may have many troubles, but the Lord delivers him from them all."

- PSALM 34:19

A teenage boy was faced with a difficult choice when he found a wallet on the street with a large amount of money inside. He knew he could keep the money and no one would know, but he also knew it wasn't right. He made the decision to turn in the wallet to the police station and was proud of himself for doing the right thing. He learned that having integrity is about doing what's right, even when no one is watching.

Reflection:

In what areas of your life do you need to prioritize integrity and honesty?

Prayer:

Dear God,

Help me to live with integrity and honesty. Give me the strength to do what is right, even when it's difficult, and the courage to stand up for my beliefs.

Amen.

30

RESPONSIBILITY

___/___/_____

"Each of you should use whatever gift you have received to serve others, as faithful stewards of God's grace in its various forms."

- I PETER 4:10

A teenage boy was asked to take care of his younger siblings while his parents were out of town. At first, he was hesitant and nervous, but he knew he had a responsibility to take care of his family. He took the job seriously and made sure his siblings were fed, bathed, and put to bed on time. When his parents returned, they praised him for his maturity and responsibility. He learned that taking responsibility is an important part of growing up and being a reliable person.

Reflection:

Are you a responsible person?

What are some ways you can take more responsibility for your actions and choices?

Prayer:

Dear God,

Help me to be a responsible person. Give me the awareness to under-stand the consequences of my choices and the courage to take responsi-bility for them.

Amen.

31

—·—

TRUSTWORTHINESS

___/___/_____

"Whoever can be trusted with very little can also be trusted with much, and whoever is dishonest with very little will also be dishonest with much."

- LUKE 16:10

B eing trustworthy means that people can rely on you to do what you say you will do. It also means being honest, even when it's hard.

This means that if we are trustworthy with small things, like keeping our promises to our friends or being honest with our parents, we will also be trustworthy in bigger things. As a teen boy, people will look up to you for guidance and leadership, so it's important to be someone that they can trust.

Reflection:

Take some time to honestly reflect - are you a trustworthy person? Why?

How can you build and maintain trust with others?

Prayer:

Dear God,

Help me to be a trustworthy person. Give me the integrity and character to keep my promises and to always act with honesty and sincerity.

Amen.

32

—·—

SELF-CONTROL

___/___/_____

"For God gave us a spirit not of fear but of power and love and self-control."

- 2 TIMOTHY 1:7

As a teen boy, you may sometimes feel like your emotions are out of control. You may feel angry or upset, and it can be hard to know what to do. But the Bible tells us that God gave us a spirit of self-control.

With God's help, we can learn to control our emotions and make wise decisions, even when we're feeling upset. It's important to remember that self-control isn't about never feeling emotions; it's about learning to manage them in a healthy way.

Reflection:

Can you think of a time you lacked self-control?

How can you develop more self-control in your thoughts, actions, and emotions?

Prayer:

Dear God,

Help me to exercise self-control in all areas of my life. Give me the wisdom to make good choices and the discipline to resist temptation.

Amen.

33

— · —

ENDURANCE

___/___/_____

"Blessed is the one who perseveres under trial because, having stood the test, that person will receive the crown of life that the Lord has promised to those who love him."

- JAMES 1:12

Endurance means sticking with something even when it's hard. As a teen boy, you may face difficult situations, whether it's a challenging school assignment or a tough sports game.

The Bible tells us that if we persevere under trial, we will receive a reward. So, if you're struggling with something right now, remember to keep going and trust that God will see you through it.

Reflection:

In what areas of your life do you need to cultivate more endurance and perseverance?

If you stick to something, you will always succeed. Never give up if you're passionate about something!

Prayer:

Dear God,

Give me the strength and endurance to face the challenges that come my way. Help me to persevere through difficult times and to never give up on my dreams and goals. Amen.

34

─ . ─

COMPASSIONATE LISTENING

___/___/_____

"My dear brothers and sisters, take note of this: Everyone should be quick to listen, slow to speak, and slow to become angry."

- JAMES 1:19

Sometimes as teen boys, it can be easy to get caught up in our own thoughts and ideas. We may not always take the time to listen to others, or we may interrupt when someone else is speaking. The Bible tells us that we should be quick to listen and slow to speak.

This means that we should take the time to really hear what others are saying, and not just wait for our turn to talk. When we practice compassionate listening, we show others that we value them and their opinions.

Reflection:

Reflect and take some time to think if you've been listening compassionately, or just waiting for your time to speak.

How can you practice listening with empathy and understanding to others?

Prayer:

Dear God,

Help me to listen with compassion and understanding to those around me. Give me the patience and willingness to understand others' perspectives and needs.

Amen.

35

— · —

ACCOUNTABILITY

___/___/_____

"Therefore confess your sins to each other and pray for each other so that you may be healed. The prayer of a righteous person is powerful and effective."

\- JAMES 5:16

As human beings, we all make mistakes. But the Bible tells us that we should confess our sins to each other and pray for each other so that we can be healed.

This can be hard to do, but it's an important part of growing in our faith and becoming better people. When we hold ourselves accountable, we show others that we're committed to living a life that honors God.

Reflection:

Who can you trust to hold me accountable and help me grow in my faith?

What other areas of your life could you benefit from being held accountable for? Perhaps in business, going to practice, or keeping up with your studies.

Prayer:

Dear God,

Thank you to the people in my life who hold me accountable and help me grow in my faith. Give me the humility to listen to their guidance, and help me to be a positive influence on others.

Amen.

36

WISE DECISION-MAKING

___ / ___ / _____

"Trust in the Lord with all your heart and lean not on your own under-standing; in all your ways submit to him, and he will make your paths straight."

- PROVERBS 3:5-6

As a teen boy, you'll be faced with many choices that will shape your future. It's important to remember that you don't have to make those decisions alone. Trust in the Lord with all your heart and lean not on your own understanding. Seek God's guidance and submit to His will, and He will make your paths straight.

Reflection:

What wise decisions have you made recently? Have you made any that weren't so wise?

How can you make wise decisions that honor God and bless others?

Prayer:

Dear God,

Give me wisdom and discernment when making decisions. Help me to seek your will and to make choices that honor you and bless others.

Amen.

37

—·—

SPIRITUAL DISCIPLINE

___/___/_____

"Do you not know that in a race, all the runners run, but only one gets the prize? Run in such a way as to get the prize. Everyone who competes in the games goes into strict training. They do it to get a crown that will not last, but we do it to get a crown that will last forever."

- I CORINTHIANS 9:24-25

J ust like athletes train their bodies to compete, we need to train our spirits to walk with God. We do this by praying, reading the Bible, and attending church. Remember that the prize we seek is eternal, so let's run in such a way as to get the prize.

Reflection:

Do you think you have strong spiritual discipline?

How can you develop your spiritual life and grow closer to God?

Prayer:

Dear God,

Help me to develop spiritual discipline in my life. Show me ways to grow closer to you, such as prayer, reading the Bible, and worship. Help me to make time for these things each day.

Amen.

38
— · —

CREATIVITY

___/___/_____

"In the beginning, God created the heavens and the earth."

— GENESIS 1:1

God is the ultimate Creator, who made the heavens and the earth. As His children, we have a spark of His creativity within us. By using our imagination and exploring different ways to express ourselves, we can tap into this creativity and bring something new into the world. Whether it's through art, music, writing, or any other form of expression, let's use our creativity to honor God and share His love with others.

Reflection:

In what ways have you been creative recently? How do you enjoy being creative?

How can you use your creativity to bring joy to others and honor God?

Prayer:

Dear God,

Thank you for the gift of creativity. Help me to use it to bring joy to others and to honor you. Give me the courage to try new things and to use my imagination for good.

Amen.

39

— . —

JOY

___/___/_____

"Rejoice always, pray continually, give thanks in all circumstances; for this is God's will for you in Christ Jesus."

- I THESSALONIANS 5:16-18

L ife can be hard, but as Christians, we have reason to rejoice always. No matter what we're going through, we can pray continually and give thanks in all circumstances, knowing that God is with us and His plans for us are good.

Reflection:

What gives you joy? When have you felt joy recently, what caused it?

How can you find joy in the midst of difficult circumstances?

Prayer:

Dear God,

Help me to find joy in all situations, even when things are tough. Remind me that true joy comes from you, and help me to focus on the blessings in my life.

Amen.

40

— . —

HONESTY

___/___/_____

"Therefore, each of you must put off falsehood and speak truthfully to your neighbor, for we are all members of one body."

- EPHESIANS 4:25

As a member of the body of Christ, honesty is essential. We must put off falsehood and speak truthfully to others. This means being honest with ourselves, with God, and with those around us.

Reflection:

Do you ever get tempted not to be honest?

How can you be honest with yourself and others, even when it's difficult?

It's important to remember, the truth *always* comes out.

Prayer:

Dear God,

Give me the strength to be honest with myself and others. Help me to speak the truth with love and kindness, and to always act with integrity.

Amen.

41

— • —

GENEROSITY

___/___/_____

"Each of you should give what you have decided in your heart to give, not reluctantly or under compulsion, for God loves a cheerful giver."

- 2 CORINTHIANS 9:7

A s followers of Christ, we're called to be generous with our time, talents, and resources. Give with a cheerful heart, knowing that everything we have comes from God and that our generosity can make a real difference in the world.

Reflection:

Reflect on your week. Have you shown anyone generosity?

In what ways can you be more generous with your time, talents, and resources?

Prayer:

Dear God,

Help us to understand that everything we have comes from you, and that we are called to be good stewards of our resources. Teach us to be generous with our time, talents, and resources, and to use them to help others. May we learn to give without expecting anything in return, and to find joy in sharing our blessings with others.

Amen.

42

— · —

Servanthood

___/___/_____

"For even the Son of Man did not come to be served, but to serve, and to give his life as a ransom for many."

- MARK 10:45

J esus came not to be served but to serve. As a teen, you may think that the world revolves around you and your desires. But just as Jesus served others, so should you. Look for opportunities to help others without expecting anything in return.

Reflection:

How can you serve those around you, whether it be your family, friends, or community?

Prayer:

Dear God,

Help us to understand that true leadership is found in serving others. Teach us to be humble and to use our abilities and resources to help those in need. May we follow your example and be willing to serve others with a willing and joyful heart.

Amen.

43

RESPECT

___/___/_____

"Show proper respect to everyone, love the family of believers, fear God, honor the emperor."

- I PETER 2:17

It's important to show respect to everyone, regardless of their status or background. This means treating others the way you want to be treated, using polite language, and being considerate of others' feelings.

Reflection:

Who do you have a lot of respect for?

In what ways can you demonstrate respect towards others, even if you don't always agree with them?

Prayer:

Dear God,

I pray for your help in showing respect to those around me. Please help me to remember that every person is created in your image and deserves to be treated with dignity and kindness.

Amen.

44

—·—

MENTAL HEALTH

___/___/_____

"Anxiety weighs down the heart, but a kind word cheers it up."

- PROVERBS 12:25

Anxiety can weigh heavily on your heart and affect your mental and physical health. Don't be afraid to talk to a trusted friend, family member, or counselor about your feelings. And always remember that God is there to comfort and guide you through any difficult times.

Reflection:

On a scale of 1-10 (1 being really bad, and 10 being amazing) - how is your mental health?

What are some healthy habits or coping mechanisms that you can incorporate into your daily routine to improve your mental health?

Prayer:

Dear God,

I pray for your guidance and support as I work to prioritize my mental health. Please help me to recognize when I need to take a break or seek help, and give me the strength to do so. Thank you for being a source of comfort and peace in difficult times.

Amen.

45

AUTHENTICITY

___/___/_____

"Therefore, if anyone is in Christ, the new creation has come: The old has gone, the new is here!"

- 2 CORINTHIANS 5:17

God has made you unique and special, so don't try to be someone you're not. Embrace your true self and strive to live a life that honors God. You don't have to be perfect, but with God's help, you can become the best version of yourself.

Reflection:

Reflect and take some time to think if you've acted differently to fit in before.

How can you embrace your true self and express it authentically to the world?

Prayer:

Dear God,

Help me to be true to myself and show the world who I really am. Help me to embrace my strengths and weaknesses and use them for your glory.

Amen.

46

—·—

REGRET

___/___/_____

"If we confess our sins, he is faithful and just and will forgive us our sins and purify us from all unrighteousness."

- I JOHN 1:9

We all make mistakes, but the important thing is to take responsibility for them and seek forgiveness. Don't let regret consume you, but use it as an opportunity to learn and grow. And remember, God is always ready to forgive when we confess our sins and turn to Him.

Reflect on any mistakes or poor choices you made during the day and ask God for forgiveness and the strength to make better choices in the future.

Reflection:

Take a moment to reflect on anything you might regret in life. How can you move past feelings of regret and learn from your mistakes?

Prayer:

Dear God,

Help me to learn from my mistakes and to move forward with grace and wisdom. Help me to let go of regret and to trust in your plan for my life.

Amen.

47

— • —

ANXIETY

___/___/_____

"Cast all your anxiety on him because he cares for you."

- I PETER 5:7

As a teen boy, you may experience anxiety about school, friendships, and the future. But remember that God cares for you and wants to help you through it. When you feel anxious or stressed about the day's events or future, take a moment to pray and give your worries to Him. Trust that He has a plan for your life and will guide you through any challenges that come your way.

Reflection:

Reflect on times you've been anxious. What was causing it?

Remember that your body can't tell the difference between anxiety and excitement, it's up to you to decide how you make sense of it. Believing you're excited will help you push through it! Trust that God will be with you every step of the way.

Prayer:

Dear God,

When I am anxious and worried, help me to turn to you for peace and comfort. Help me to trust in your love and care for me, and to know that you are always with me.

Amen.

48

— • —

PRIDE

___/___/_____

"When pride comes, then comes disgrace, but with humility comes wisdom."

- PROVERBS 11:2

Pride can be a stumbling block in your relationships with others and with God. Remember that true wisdom comes from humility, not arrogance.

Reflection:

Reflect on times when you've let pride or arrogance get in the way of your relationships, and ask God to help you cultivate a humble heart.

How can you avoid the trap of pride in the future?

Prayer:

Dear God,

Help me to avoid the sin of pride and to cultivate humility in my thoughts and actions. Help me to recognize and appreciate the gifts and talents of others, and to use my own talents for the greater good.

Amen.

49

— · —

SLOTH

___/___/_____

"Whatever you do, work at it with all your heart, as working for the Lord, not for human masters."

- COLOSSIANS 3:23

As a young man, it's important to take responsibility for your actions and work hard in all that you do. Remember that everything you do is ultimately for the Lord, not just for your own benefit. If you struggle with laziness or procrastination, pray for God's strength and motivation to help you work diligently and with purpose.

Reflection:

Reflect on any areas where you procrastinated during the day and ask God for the motivation and energy to be productive in the future.

Prayer:

Dear God,

Please help me to avoid the sin of sloth so I can become more proactive and productive in life.

Amen.

50

— . —

LAZINESS

___/___/_____

"Lazy hands make for poverty, but diligent hands bring wealth."

- PROVERBS 10:4

Laziness may seem tempting in the moment, but it can lead to poverty and missed opportunities. Instead, strive to be diligent and hardworking in all aspects of your life. Ask God to help you develop a strong work ethic and the discipline to follow through on your commitments.

Reflection:

Look back over the last couple of weeks. Do you think you've been lazy?

How can you overcome this laziness and become more productive?

Prayer:

Dear God,

Give me the motivation and energy to pursue my goals and dreams. Help me to overcome any tendencies towards laziness or procrastination and to be diligent in my work.

Amen.

51

—·—

UNFORGIVENESS

___/___/_____

"Be kind and compassionate to one another, forgiving each other, just as in Christ God forgave you."

- EPHESIANS 4:32

F orgiveness can be difficult, especially when someone has hurt you deeply. But as a follower of Christ, we are called to be kind and compassionate to others, even when it's hard. Remember that God has forgiven you, and extend that same forgiveness to those who have wronged you. It's not always easy, but it's necessary for your own emotional and spiritual health.

Reflection:

Take a moment to think if there's anyone who has hurt you so deeply that you can't forgive them.

How can you let go of anger and bitterness towards them and others who have wronged you?

Prayer:

Dear God,

Help me to release any unforgiveness in my heart towards those who have hurt me. Help me to understand that forgiveness is a process and guide me towards healing and peace.

Amen.

52

— . —

DISCERNMENT

___/___/_____

"Beloved, do not believe every spirit, but test the spirits to see whether they are from God, for many false prophets have gone out into the world."

- I JOHN 4:1

D iscernment is the ability to judge well, to separate truth from falsehood, and to make wise decisions. It is important to ask God for discernment, especially when facing difficult choices or temptations. By seeking God's wisdom and guidance, we can avoid making decisions that may harm ourselves or others.

Reflection:

Do you think you have good judgment?

How can you develop your ability to discern right from wrong?

Prayer:

Dear God,

Give me the wisdom and discernment to make good choices and decisions in my life. Help me to be aware of the consequences of my actions and to seek your guidance in all that I do.

Amen.

53

— · —

JUSTICE

___/___/_____

"Learn to do good; seek justice, correct oppression; bring justice to the father-less, plead the widow's cause."

- ISAIAH 1:17

God cares deeply about justice, and as His followers, we should too. It is important to stand up for what is right and to advocate for those who are marginalized or oppressed. Whether it is speaking out against bullying or injustice, or supporting organizations that work toward social justice, we can all make a difference in our communities.

Reflection:

How can you promote justice in your daily life and actions?

Prayer:

Dear God,

Help me to seek justice in my life and stand up for what is right. Guide me to use my voice and actions to bring about change and make a positive impact in the world.

Amen.

54

PERFECTIONISM

___/___/_____

"Not that I have already obtained this or am already perfect, but I press on to make it my own, because Christ Jesus has made me his own."

- PHILIPPIANS 3:12

While it is important to strive for excellence in all that we do, it is also important to recognize that we are not perfect and that we all make mistakes. Perfectionism can lead to feelings of anxiety, stress, and inadequacy, but we can find peace and freedom by embracing our imperfections and focusing on growth and progress instead.

Reflection:

In what ways does perfectionism hold you back and prevent you from fully living?

We learn from mistakes. How can you move forward being okay with making them?

Prayer:

Dear God,

Please help me break free from the chains of perfectionism. Let me release my grip on control and instead trust in your perfect plan for my life. Help me to find joy in the journey rather than the destination, and let me embrace the beauty of imperfection.

Amen.

55

— . —

PEACE

___/___/_____

"the peace of God, which transcends all understanding, will guard your hearts and your minds in Christ Jesus."

- PHILIPPIANS 4:6-7

I n a world filled with chaos and uncertainty, God offers us peace that surpasses all understanding. We can find this peace by spending time in prayer and by seeking God's presence in our lives. By trusting in God's goodness and faithfulness, we can find comfort and rest in the midst of life's challenges.

Reflection:

How can I cultivate a sense of peace in my heart and mind amidst the chaos of life?

Prayer:

Dear God,

Help me trust in you and find rest in your presence. Let me release my anxieties and worries to you, and let my heart and mind be filled with your peace.

Amen

56

— . —

ENCOURAGEMENT

___/___/_____

"Therefore encourage one another and build each other up, just as in fact
you are doing."

- I THESSALONIANS 5:II

E ncouragement is a powerful tool that we can use to uplift and inspire those around us. Whether it is through a kind word, a listening ear, or a thoughtful gesture, we can all make a difference in someone's life. By showing others that we care and that we believe in them, we can help them to reach their full potential.

Reflection:

Take a moment to reflect on the last time you encouraged someone, or they encouraged you. What did they say? Did it work?

Prayer:

Dear God,

Show me ways to uplift and inspire those around me, and let my words and actions bring hope and joy. Let me be a reflection of your love and grace.

Amen.

57
— · —

ADVENTURE

___/___/_____

"For I know the plans I have for you," declares the Lord, "plans to prosper you and not to harm you, plans to give you hope and a future."

- JEREMIAH 29:11

L ife is an adventure, and God has created us to live it to the fullest. Whether it is trying something new, taking risks, or pursuing our passions, we can embrace the spirit of adventure and discover all that life has to offer. By trusting in God's plan for our lives and stepping out in faith, we can experience the thrill of the unknown and grow in ways we never thought possible.

Reflection:

When was the last time you tried something new, took a risk, or pursued your passion?

How can you step out of your comfort zone and experience new adventures that will help you grow?

Prayer:

Dear God,

Thank you for the gift of life and the opportunities to experience new adventures. Help me to trust in you as I step out of my comfort zone and take risks. Let me be open to new experiences and the growth that comes with them. Keep me safe and guide me as I journey through life.

Amen.

58

—.—

AUTHENTICITY

___/___/_____

"Therefore, if anyone is in Christ, the new creation has come: The old has gone, the new is here!"

- 2 CORINTHIANS 5:17

I n a world where everyone is trying to fit in, be different. God made you unique and special, so embrace your individuality and be true to yourself.

Reflection:

In what ways can I be more authentic in my relationships with others and with God?

Prayer:

Dear God,

Help me live a life of authenticity and vulnerability. Let me be honest with myself and others, and let me embrace who you created me to be. Help me to not fear judgment or rejection, but to trust in your love and acceptance.

Amen.

59

— · —

COMMUNITY

___/___/_____

"For where two or three gather in my name, there am I with them."

- MATTHEW 18:20

Life is not meant to be lived alone. We need the support and encouragement of others to grow and thrive. Build genuine relationships with others and invest in your community.

Reflection:

Do you have a good community around you?

How can you serve and support those around you in your community?

Prayer:

Dear God,

Thank you for the gift of community and the people you have placed in my life. Help me love and serve them well, and show me ways to be a light in their lives. Let my actions reflect your love and grace, and let my words bring encouragement and hope.

Amen.

60

— · —

PERFECTION

___/___/_____

"Be perfect, therefore, as your heavenly Father is perfect."

- MATTHEW 5:48

S triving for excellence is admirable, but don't let the pursuit of perfection hold you back. Recognize that everyone makes mistakes, and it's okay to fall short sometimes. Learn from your mistakes and keep moving forward.

Reflection:

How does your pursuit of perfectionism affect your relationships with others and your relationship with God?

Prayer:

Dear God,

Please help me release my grip on perfectionism and instead embrace the beauty of imperfection. Help me remember that my worth is found in you alone and not in my achievements or abilities.

Amen.

61

— · —

RISK-TAKING

___/___/_____

"For God gave us a spirit not of fear but of power and love and self-control."

- 2 TIMOTHY 1:7

Taking risks can be scary, but it's often necessary to achieve our goals and dreams in life. Don't let fear hold you back from stepping out of your comfort zone and trying new things, whether that be your faith, relationships, or goals. Trust that God is with you every step of the way.

Reflection:

When was the last time you took a risk in life?

What is one area in your life where you can step out of your comfort zone and take a risk?

Prayer:

Dear God,

Please give me the courage and wisdom to take risks that honor you and lead me to new opportunities. Help me trust in your plans and guidance, and let my actions bring glory to your name.

Amen.

62

— . —

INNOVATION

___/___/_____

"See, I am doing a new thing! Now it springs up; do you not perceive it? I am making a way in the wilderness and streams in the wasteland."

- ISAIAH 43:19

G od has given us all unique talents and abilities. Use them to create, innovate, and make a positive impact on the world around you.

Reflection:

Take a moment to think of any great ideas you may have had recently.

How can you use your creativity and innovation to make a positive impact in the world for yourself or others?

Prayer:

Dear God,

Grant me the wisdom and creativity to innovate in ways that honor you and benefit others. Help me to use my talents and gifts to make a positive difference in the world.

Amen.

63

— • —

SIMPLICITY

___/___/_____

"But seek first his kingdom and his righteousness, and all these things will be given to you as well."

I n a world full of noise and distractions, learn to appreciate the simple things in life. Take time to slow down and enjoy the beauty around you.

Reflection:

Do you take enough time to appreciate the little things in life? Take a moment to slow down and enjoy them.

Prayer:

Dear God,

Guide me in simplifying my life and letting go of any distractions or excess that may be holding me back. Help me to focus on what truly matters and to prioritize my relationship with you above all else.

Amen.

64

— • —

EXERCISE

___/___/_____

"Do you not know that your bodies are temples of the Holy Spirit, who is in you, whom you have received from God?"

- I CORINTHIANS 6:19

Taking care of your physical health is important, not just for your body, but also for your mind and spirit. Make exercise a regular part of your routine and prioritize your overall health and wellness. Your bodies are a gift from God - it's beautiful to see what your body is truly capable of; you'd be surprised!

Reflection:

Take a moment to reflect and ask yourself if you're exercising enough each day.

How can I incorporate regular exercise into my routine to improve my physical health and well-being?

Prayer:

Dear God,

Help me to make exercise a regular part of my life so that I may honor you with a healthy body and mind. Grant me the energy and motivation to make it a priority.

Amen.

65

— • —

DISCIPLINE

___/___/_____

"I discipline my body like an athlete, training it to do what it should."

- I CORINTHIANS 9:27

A s Jim Rohn said, Discipline is the bridge between goals and accomplishment. It's important to remember that discipline is not punishment, but rather a tool to help us reach our goals and achieve success. It takes discipline to develop good habits, practice self-control, and maintain a positive attitude, but the results are worth it.

Reflection:

In what ways do you show discipline to ensure you accomplish your goals?

In what areas of your life do you need to develop greater discipline and self-control?

Prayer:

Dear God,

Help me to develop the discipline I need to achieve my goals and live according to your will. Grant me the perseverance to overcome any challenges or obstacles that may arise.

Amen.

66

—.—

HEALTH

___/___/_____

"Dear friend, I pray that you may enjoy good health and that all may go well with you, even as your soul is getting along well."

- 3 JOHN 1:2

O ur physical and mental health are precious gifts from God. We should take care of our bodies by eating well, exercising regularly, and getting enough sleep. When we prioritize our health, we are better able to serve God and others.

Reflection:

Take a moment to reflect on how well you take care of your health.

How can you honor God with your body by living a healthy lifestyle and making wise choices?

Prayer:

Dear God,

Guide me in making choices that honor and glorify you, including those related to my health. Grant me the motivation and strength to take care of my body as a temple of your Holy Spirit.

Amen.

67

— . —

SELF-CARE

___/___/_____

"Love your neighbor as yourself."

We often focus on loving others and forget to take care of ourselves. Self-care is an important part of loving our neighbor because when we are healthy and happy, we are better equipped to serve and help others.

Reflection:

Do you take good care of yourself?

In what ways can you prioritize your mental, physical, spiritual, and emotional health and well-being?

Prayer:

Dear God,

Help me to recognize the importance of self-care and to make it a priority in my life. Grant me the strength to take care of my mind, body, and spirit so that I may better serve you and others.

Amen.

68

---·---

MODERATION

___/___/_____

"Do not be among those who give themselves to wine or gluttonous feasts. For drunkards and gluttons become poor, and drowsiness clothes them in rags."

- PROVERBS 23:20-21

It's important to find a balance between indulging in what we enjoy and practicing self-control. Too much of anything can be harmful, but depriving ourselves of things we love can also be detrimental to our well-being.

Reflection:

Think of some ways you may or may not have moderation in life.

How can you practice moderation in all aspects of your life and avoid excess and extremes?

Prayer:

Dear God,

Grant me the self-control to live a balanced life and avoid any harmful habits or behaviors. Help me to find contentment in moderation and to use my resources wisely.

Amen.

69

— • —

SELF-IMPROVEMENT

___/___/_____

"Let us not become weary in doing good, for at the proper time we will reap a harvest if we do not give up."

— GALATIANS 6:9

We can't change the world around us until we change ourselves. Self-improvement is a life-long journey of personal growth and development, and it requires us to be intentional and consistent in our efforts to become the best versions of ourselves.

All you need to do is become 1% better, every day. Check out 'Hamza' or '1STMAN' on youtube for more detailed advice.

Reflection:

Take a moment to think about where you'd like to improve in your life.

In what ways can you grow and improve as a person while staying true to your values and beliefs?

Prayer:

Dear God,

Help me to recognize my strengths and weaknesses and guide me as I strive to become the best version of myself. Grant me the wisdom to make positive changes in my life and the courage to overcome any obstacles in my path.

Amen.

70

—·—

BALANCE

___/___/_____

"For everything, there is a season and a time for every matter under heaven."

- ECCLESIASTES 3:1

L ife is full of ups and downs, and it's important to find a balance between work and play, rest and activity, and giving and receiving. When we strive for balance in our lives, we can find peace and contentment.

Reflection:

Take a moment to reflect on your life. Do you think you have a good balance?

In what areas of your life do you need to find more balance?

Prayer:

Dear God,

Help me to find balance in my life between work and rest, responsibility and leisure, and all of the other areas that demand my attention. Grant me the wisdom to prioritize what is truly important and to let go of what is not.

Amen.

71

—·—

OVERCOMING NEGATIVE SELF-TALK

___/___/_____

"Do not be conformed to this world, but be transformed by the renewal of your mind, that by testing you may discern what is the will of God, what is good and acceptable and perfect."

- ROMANS 12:2

Negative self-talk can be a difficult cycle to break. It can be so easy to listen to the lies we tell ourselves, and sometimes we don't even realize we're doing it. But God's Word reminds us that we don't have to conform to those negative thoughts. We have the power to transform our minds and replace those lies with truth. We can renew our minds with the Word of God and by testing those negative thoughts against what is good, acceptable, and perfect according to His will. As we do so, we'll find ourselves growing in confidence and overcoming the negative self-talk that once held us back.

Reflection:

Take some time to reflect – would you say you have positive or negative self-talk? What do you say to yourself?

How can you change your inner dialogue to be more positive and up-lifting?

Prayer:

Dear God,

Help me to recognize negative self-talk when it arises and to replace it with positive and affirming thoughts. Grant me the strength to see myself as you see me, and to embrace the love and grace that you offer me.

Amen.

72

BREAKING FREE FROM ADDICTION

___/___/_____

"It is for freedom that Christ has set us free. Stand firm, then, and do not let yourselves be burdened again by a yoke of slavery."

- GALATIANS 5:1

Addiction can be a powerful force, but with faith, determination, and support, we can overcome it. Breaking free from addiction requires courage, humility, and a willingness to seek help and change our behavior. But with God's help, we can find freedom and hope.

Reflection:

Do you have addictive behaviors that you can't seem to stop? Have you seen anyone else with them?

What steps can you take to break free from addictive behaviors?

Prayer:

Dear God,

I ask for your help and guidance as I work to overcome addiction. Please grant me the strength and willpower to make positive changes in my life, and to turn to you for support and encouragement.

Amen.

73

—.—

FINDING PEACE IN THE MIDST OF CHAOS

___/___/_____

"Do not be anxious about anything, but in every situation, by prayer and petition, with thanksgiving, present your requests to God. And the peace of God, which transcends all understanding, will guard your hearts and your minds in Christ Jesus."

- PHILIPPIANS 4:6-7

L ife can be chaotic and overwhelming at times, especially in today's fast-paced world. But even in the midst of chaos, there is an opportunity to find peace. By focusing on God's presence and trusting in His plan, we can experience a sense of calm and comfort. Remember that peace is not the absence of chaos, but rather the ability to remain calm and centered in the midst of it. Take time to pray, meditate, and connect with God daily to cultivate inner peace and find the strength to navigate life's challenges.

Reflection:

Take a moment to reflect on your life. Are you currently at peace, or is there chaos?

What practices can you incorporate into your life to find peace amidst chaos?

Prayer:

Dear God,

In moments of chaos and stress, please grant me the peace and calmness that only you can provide. Help me to surrender my worries to you and to trust in your plan for my life.

Amen.

74

—·—

FINDING STRENGTH IN GOD DURING PHYSICAL CHALLENGES

___/___/_____

"I can do all this through him who gives me strength."

- PHILIPPIANS 4:13

L ife is full of physical challenges, whether it be in sports/activities, illness, injury, or disability. In times like these, we may feel weak and vulnerable, but we can find strength in God. We can trust that He is with us and will give us the strength we need to face our challenges.

Reflection:

When was the last time you had a physical challenge?

How can you lean on God during times of physical struggle?

Prayer:

Dear God,

In times of physical pain or illness, please grant me the strength and comfort to endure. Help me to trust in your plan for my life, and to find peace and hope in your love for me.

Amen.

75

—·—

RESILIENCE

___/___/_____

"Consider it pure joy, my brothers and sisters, whenever you face trials of many kinds because you know that the testing of your faith produces perseverance."

- JAMES 1:2-3

Life is full of ups and downs. We will face setbacks and challenges, but we can learn to be resilient. Resilience is the ability to bounce back from adversity and to keep moving forward. We can develop resilience by trusting in God's plan, staying positive, and seeking support from others.

Reflection:

Reflect on a moment you faced a setback or challenge. Did you stay resilient, or give up?

What are some ways you can build your resilience in the face of challenges?

Prayer:

Dear God,

Help me to have the strength and perseverance to overcome challenges and to trust in your plan for my life. Give me the courage to keep moving forward even when things get difficult. Amen.

76

— • —

MINDFULNESS

___/___/_____

"Finally, brothers and sisters, whatever is true, whatever is noble, whatever is right, whatever is pure, whatever is lovely, whatever is admirable--if anything is excellent or praiseworthy--think about such things."

- PHILIPPIANS 4:8

In a world full of distractions, it can be easy to lose focus and become overwhelmed. Mindfulness is the practice of being present in the moment and paying attention to our thoughts and feelings. We can cultivate mindfulness by taking time to be still, practicing deep breathing, and being intentional about our thoughts and actions.

Reflection:

Take a moment to reflect on your day. Are you being mindful?

How can you cultivate a more mindful and present attitude in your daily life?

Prayer:

Dear God,

Help me to be fully present in each moment, and to find joy in the simple pleasures of life. Guide me in being more mindful of your presence in all things.

Amen.

77

— . —

NUTRITION

___/___/_____

"Do you not know that your bodies are temples of the Holy Spirit, who is in you, whom you have received from God? You are not your own"

- 1 CORINTHIANS 6:19

Our bodies need proper nutrition to function at their best. We should strive to eat a balanced diet, including plenty of fruits, vegetables, and whole grains. When we nourish our bodies, we are better able to serve God and others.

Reflection:

Reflect on the foods you eat. Do you eat healthy enough?

How can you make healthier food choices to nourish your body and mind?

Prayer:

Dear God,

Guide me in making wise choices about what I eat and drink. Help me to take care of my body and honor you with the choices I make.

Amen.

78

─ · ─

SLEEP

___/___/_____

"In vain, you rise early and stay up late, toiling for food to eat—for he grants sleep to those he loves."

- PSALM 127:2

G etting enough sleep is needed to help support our physical and mental health. When we get enough sleep, we are more alert, focused, and productive. We should make it a priority to get enough sleep each night and to create a restful sleep environment.

Reflection:

Are you going to bed early enough to feel fresh and energized each morning?

How can you prioritize getting enough restful sleep in my daily routine, and what changes can you make to improve your sleep habits?

Prayer:

Dear God,

Bless me with restful sleep each night so that I can be fully present and energized to serve you and others each day.

Amen.

79

—·—

GROWTH

___/___/_____

"Do not conform to the pattern of this world, but be transformed by the renewing of your mind."

- ROMANS 12:2

We are all works in progress. We should strive to grow in our faith, character, and relationships. We can grow by reading the Bible, seeking wise counsel, and stepping out of our comfort zones.

Reflection:

We all have areas to improve on in our lives.

In what areas of your life do you need to grow and improve, and what steps can you take to make progress?

Prayer:

Dear God,

Help me to embrace growth and change in my life. Give me the courage to face challenges and the strength to persevere through difficult times.

Amen.

80

— • —

PURPOSE

___/___/_____

"For I know the plans I have for you," declares the Lord, "plans to prosper you and not to harm you, plans to give you hope and a future."

- JEREMIAH 29:11

We all have a unique purpose in life. We should seek God's guidance to discover our purpose and to use our gifts and talents to serve others. When we live with purpose, we find greater joy and fulfillment in life.

Men will often fall into harmful activities if they do not have a purpose/mission to keep them grounded and moving toward a goal.

Reflection:

Your purpose can change throughout your life. Do you currently have a purpose/mission to focus on? It could be anything from focusing on your studies, becoming the best guitar player you can, or starting a business.

How can you use your talents and gifts to make a positive impact on the world?

Prayer:

Dear God,

Guide me in discovering my purpose in life. Help me to use my talents and gifts for your glory and to serve others with love and compassion.

Amen.

81

— · —

LOYALTY

___/___/_____

"Let love and faithfulness never leave you; bind them around your neck, write them on the tablet of your heart."

— PROVERBS 3:3

Loyalty is a powerful force in any relationship. It means standing by someone's side no matter what, through the good times and the bad. It means being there for your friends and family when they need you the most. Loyalty is about being a reliable and trustworthy person. Just like how a dog is loyal to its owner, we can learn from them and show loyalty to our loved ones.

Reflection:

Have you, or someone you know, not been loyal in the past?

In what ways can you be more loyal to your family, friends, and community?

Prayer:

Dear God,

Help me to be a faithful and loyal friend to those around me. Show me how to support and encourage others, even in difficult times.

Amen.

82

— · —

GRACIOUSNESS

___/___/_____

"Therefore, as God's chosen people, holy and dearly loved, clothe yourselves with compassion, kindness, humility, gentleness, and patience."

- COLOSSIANS 3:12

Being gracious means being kind and showing compassion even when it's difficult or undeserved. It's important to remember that everyone makes mistakes and has bad days. Instead of reacting with anger or judgment, choose to respond with understanding and forgiveness. By showing grace, you not only make a positive impact on others but also cultivate a sense of inner peace and contentment.

Reflection:

How can we show more grace towards others in our daily interactions?

Prayer:

Dear God,

Help me to show grace to others, even when it's difficult. Give me the strength to forgive and love as you do.

Amen.

83

— • —

PRESENCE

___/___/_____

"This is the day that the Lord has made; let us rejoice and be glad in it."

- PSALM 118:24

I n a world full of distractions, it's easy to lose sight of what really matters. Being present means focusing on what's in front of you, whether it's spending time with family, doing your school work, or just enjoying a moment of solitude. When you're present, you can fully engage with the world around you and experience life in a deeper way.

Reflection:

Take a moment to be present and grateful for the blessings in your life today.

How can we be fully present in our relationships with others, and with God?

Prayer:

Dear God,

Help us to be fully present in each moment, and to give our undivided attention to those around us. May we also be present to your voice and leading in our lives.

Amen.

84

—.—

STILLNESS

___/___/_____

"Be still and know that I am God."

- PSALM 46:10

In the midst of a busy life, it's important to find moments of stillness. Whether it's through prayer, meditation, or simply taking a few deep breaths, stillness can help you reconnect with yourself and with God. In these quiet moments, you can find peace, clarity, and a renewed sense of purpose.

Reflection:

Take a moment to be still and listen for God's voice in your life.

In a world that is constantly on the go, how can we find stillness and rest in God's presence?

Prayer:

Dear God,

Help us to slow down and be still in your presence. May we find rest and peace in you, and be renewed in body, mind, and spirit.

Amen.

85

— · —

AWARENESS

___/___/_____

"The Lord is my shepherd; I lack nothing. He makes me lie down in green pastures and leads me beside quiet waters."

- PSALM 23:1-2

It's easy to get caught up in our own thoughts and feelings, but being aware of the world around us can bring a sense of peace and connection. By being aware of what's around you, you can learn to appreciate the present moment and find joy in the simple things.

Reflection:

Take a moment to be aware of the beauty of nature around you and the peace that comes from being in God's presence.

How can we cultivate greater awareness of God's presence in our lives and in the world around us?

Prayer:

Dear God,

Open our eyes and hearts to the beauty of your creation, and help us to be aware of your presence in our lives. May we see the world through your eyes.

Amen.

86

— · —

Focus

___/___/_____

"Set your minds on things above, not on earthly things."

- Colossians 3:2

In a world filled with distractions, it can be challenging to stay focused on what's important. But when we learn to focus our attention on one thing at a time, we can be more productive and achieve our goals. By focusing your energy and attention, you can accomplish great things. Prioritize what's important in your life and develop a plan to achieve it.

Reflection:

Take a moment to think about your day. Have you been focused on your daily tasks, or has your attention been elsewhere?

How can we focus on the things that truly matter, rather than getting distracted by the noise and busyness of life?

Prayer:

Dear God,

Help us to keep our eyes fixed on you and your purposes for our lives. Give us the strength and discipline to focus on what is truly important.

Amen.

87

— · —

SURRENDER

___/___/_____

"Trust in the Lord with all your heart and lean not on your own under-standing; in all your ways submit to him, and he will make your paths straight."

- PROVERBS 3:5-6

Sometimes we try to control everything in our lives, but it's important to recognize that some things are out of our control. Learning to surrender to the universe or a higher power can bring a sense of peace and trust in the process of life. Surrendering doesn't mean giving up or not trying, but rather letting go of the need to control every outcome. Trust that everything happens for a reason and that things will work out in the end.

Reflection:

What areas in our lives are we struggling to surrender to God? Are you trying to control exactly how your life goes?

Take a moment to surrender your worries and fears to God and trust that He will guide you in the right direction.

Prayer:

Dear God,

Help us to let go of our fears and worries, and surrender control to you. May we trust in your perfect plan for our lives.

Amen.

88

— · —

ACCEPTANCE

___/___/_____

"For God did not send his Son into the world to condemn the world, but to save the world through him."

- JOHN 3:17

L ife is full of ups and downs, and sometimes things don't go as planned. But by practicing acceptance, we can find peace and move forward. Accepting a situation doesn't mean we have to like it or agree with it, but it means acknowledging it and learning to let go of any negative emotions attached to it. By accepting what we cannot change, we can focus on what we can control and find new opportunities for growth.

Reflection:

Take a moment to accept God's grace and forgiveness and let go of any shame or guilt.

How can we learn to accept ourselves and others as they are, despite our differences and flaws?

Prayer:

Dear God,

Grant us the serenity to accept the things we cannot change, the courage to change the things we can, and the wisdom to know the difference.

Amen.

89

— • —

HOPE IN ADVERSITY

___/___/_____

"We also glory in our sufferings, because we know that suffering produces perseverance; perseverance, character; and character, hope."

- ROMANS 5:3-4

L ife can be challenging, and we all face difficult situations at times. But even in the darkest moments, there is always hope. Holding onto hope allows us to see beyond our current circumstances and believe that things will get better. It's important to remember that no matter how bad things may seem, there is always a light at the end of the tunnel.

Reflection:

Think of a challenging or difficult situation you've been in. Did you hold onto hope knowing it'll all get better eventually?

How can you hold onto hope in difficult circumstances?

Prayer:

Dear God,

In times of adversity, help us to cling to the hope we have in you. May we trust in your love and provision, even when the road ahead is uncertain.

Amen.

90

— · —

TRUST IN GOD'S PLAN

___/___/_____

"For I know the plans I have for you," declares the Lord, "plans to prosper you and not to harm you, plans to give you hope and a future."

- JEREMIAH 29:11

Sometimes we may feel lost or uncertain about the future, but it's important to trust in God's plan. When we trust that everything happens for a reason and that God has a plan for us, we can find peace and direction. Trusting in God's plan doesn't mean we sit back and do nothing, but rather that we work towards our goals with faith and confidence that everything will work out according to His plan.

Reflection:

Do you trust in God's plan for you?

How can you deepen your trust in God's plan for your life?

Prayer:

Dear God,

Help us to trust in your plan for our lives, even when it is difficult or unclear. Give us the patience and faith to wait for your perfect timing and to follow your lead.

Amen.

91

— · —

OVERCOMING FEAR

___/___/_____

"So do not fear, for I am with you; do not be dismayed, for I am your God. I will strengthen you and help you; I will uphold you with my righteous right hand."

- ISAIAH 41:10

Fear can be crippling, and it can hold us back from experiencing all that God has planned for us. However, when we face our fears head-on, we can overcome them with the help of God. Trusting in God's strength and protection can give us the courage we need to face any challenge.

Reflection:

Has there been a time when you've been frightened to do something, like a speech in front of your school? How did you overcome it?

What fears are holding you back from pursuing your dreams?

Prayer:

Dear God,

Help us to overcome our fears and trust in you. Give us the strength and courage to face our fears and to pursue the plans you have for our lives.

Amen.

92

— · —

THE POWER OF PRAYER

___/___/_____

"Do not be anxious about anything, but in every situation, by prayer and petition, with thanksgiving, present your requests to God."

- PHILIPPIANS 4:6

A prayer is a powerful tool that connects us to God and strengthens our faith. It allows us to share our hopes, fears, and struggles with Him, and to receive guidance and comfort in return. By making prayer a regular part of our daily routine, we can experience a deeper relationship with God and a greater sense of peace and purpose in our lives.

Reflection:

Have you prayed recently?

How has prayer made a difference in your life?

Prayer:

Dear God,

We thank you for the power of prayer and the way it connects us to you. Help us to make prayer a priority in our lives and to trust in your answers to our prayers.

Amen.

93

— . —

RESILIENCE THROUGH FAITH

___/___/_____

"I have told you these things, so that in me you may have peace. In this world, you will have trouble. But take heart! I have overcome the world."

- JOHN 16:33

L ife is full of challenges, but when we place our faith in God, we can become more resilient and better equipped to handle whatever comes our way. By trusting in His plan for our lives and relying on His strength, we can face adversity with courage and perseverance.

Reflection:

How has your faith helped you overcome challenges in the past?

How can it help you overcome challenges in the future?

Prayer:

Dear God,

In times of struggle and adversity, give us the resilience to continue to put our faith in you. Help us to trust that you are with us every step of the way and that you will provide us with the strength to endure.

Amen.

94

MOVING FORWARD

___/___/_____

"Forgetting what is behind and straining toward what is ahead, I press on toward the goal to win the prize for which God has called me heavenward in Christ Jesus."

- PHILIPPIANS 3:13-14

Life is a journey, and sometimes we may feel stuck or unsure of which direction to take. But by staying focused on our goals, keeping our faith strong, and taking one step at a time, we can move forward with confidence and purpose.

Reflection:

What is one step you took today to move forward toward your goals?

What is one step you can take tomorrow?

How can you move forward by 1% every day?

Prayer:

Dear God,

Give us the strength and courage to move forward toward your will for our lives. Help us to trust in your plan and take action in faith.

Amen.

95

— · —

TRUE SUCCESS

___/___/_____

"And we know that in all things God works for the good of those who love him, who have been called according to his purpose."

- ROMANS 8:28

S uccess is often defined by worldly achievements like wealth, fame, or power, and material possessions. While those aren't bad and shouldn't put you off from aiming to achieve them, true success comes from living a life of purpose and meaning, following God's plan for our lives, and serving others with love and compassion.

Reflection:

What does true success mean to you, and how can you pursue it?

Prayer:

Dear God,

Guide us in our pursuit of true success, which comes from living a life that honors you and serves others. Help us to focus on what truly matters and find joy in your presence.

Amen.

96
— . —

GROWTH MINDSET

___/___/_____

"But grow in the grace and knowledge of our Lord and Savior Jesus Christ.
To him be glory both now and forever! Amen."

- 2 PETER 3:18

The way we view challenges and setbacks can have a big impact on our ability to grow and learn. By adopting a growth mindset, we can see obstacles as opportunities for growth and transformation, and become more resilient and adaptable as a result. Through faith, we can trust that God is with us every step of the way and has a plan for our growth and development.

Let's cultivate a growth mindset and be open to learning and growing.

Reflection:

How can you adopt a growth mindset and embrace challenges as opportunities for growth?

What kind of person do you want to grow into?

Prayer:

Dear God,

Help us to develop a growth mindset and trust in your plan for our lives. May we be open to new experiences and challenges, knowing that you are with us every step of the way.

Amen.

97

---.---

TEMPTATIONS OF THE ONLINE WORLD

___/___/_____

"Set your minds on things above, not on earthly things."

- COLOSSIANS 3:2

There are many temptations on the internet, such as inappropriate content, cyberbullying, or wasting time on social media. But with God's help, we can resist these temptations and make positive choices online. Let's keep our minds focused on what's truly important and use technology in positive, uplifting ways that honor God.

Reflection:

What temptations do you face when using technology, and how do you resist them?

How can you make it easier to resist them? Could you delete certain apps?

Prayer:

Dear God,

Give us the strength to resist the temptations of the online world. Help us to use technology in ways that honor you and serve others.

Amen.

98

—·—

THE IMPACT OF SOCIAL MEDIA

___/___/_____

"The tongue has the power of life and death, and those who love it will eat its fruit."

- PROVERBS 18:21

Social media can be a great way to connect with friends and family, but it can also have a negative impact on your mental health. It can give you unrealistic views of other people's lives (they only share the best bits), expose you to bullying, and rumor spreading, and even ruin your sleep (sleep is a superpower!).

Reflection:

Spend some time reflecting on how social media affects your mood and self-esteem, and consider taking a break if you feel overwhelmed or anxious.

How has social media influenced your self-image or your interactions with others?

Prayer:

Dear God,

Help us use social media in a way that glorifies you and blesses others.
May we always be mindful of the impact it has on our thoughts and
actions. Amen.

99

— · —

VALUING REAL-LIFE RELATIONSHIPS

___/___/_____

"A friend loves at all times, and a brother is born for a time of adversity."

- Proverbs 17:17

While social media can connect us with people around the world, it is important to remember the value of real-life relationships. We should strive to build strong, healthy relationships with the people in our lives and use social media as a tool to support and strengthen those relationships.

Reflection:

Are you investing enough time and effort into building and maintaining meaningful relationships in your life outside of social media? If not, what steps can you take to change this?

Prayer:

Dear God,

Help me to prioritize real-life relationships over online connections. Show me how to love and serve those in my life with the same grace and compassion you have shown me.

Amen.

100

—.—

AVOID COMPARISON ON SOCIAL MEDIA

___/___/_____

"But the Lord said to Samuel, 'Do not consider his appearance or his height, for I have rejected him. The Lord does not look at the things people look at. People look at the outward appearance, but the Lord looks at the heart.'"

- I SAMUEL 16:7 (NIV)

Social media can often create feelings of jealousy or inadequacy as we compare ourselves to others. We must remember that we are fearfully and wonderfully made by God and that our worth does not come from our online presence or popularity.

Reflection:

How can you use social media to connect with others and share your own unique experiences without comparing yourself to others?

Prayer:

Dear God,

Help me to find my worth and identity in you, and not in the opinions or status updates of others. Guide me to use social media in a way that honors you and uplifts those around me.

Amen.

101

— · —

Importance of Boundaries with Technology

___/___/_____

"Therefore do not let sin reign in your mortal body so that you obey its evil desires."

- Romans 6:12

Technology is a wonderful tool that can be used for good, but it's important to set boundaries and use it wisely. It's easy to get lost in the endless scrolling, mindless browsing, and temptation to engage in inappropriate content. Make a conscious effort to use technology in a way that aligns with your values and faith. Consider setting limits on your screen time, avoid websites and apps that promote negativity or sinful behavior, and use technology to uplift and encourage others. Remember that what you consume online can affect your thoughts, actions, and attitudes.

Reflection:

Reflect on the amount of time you spend using technology each day. Are there areas where you could cut back and focus on other activities or relationships that are important to you? How can you ensure it doesn't become a distraction or negative influence in your life?

Prayer:

Dear God,

Help me to recognize when technology is becoming a hindrance to my spiritual growth and personal development. Guide me to set healthy boundaries that allow me to use technology in a positive and productive way.

Amen.

102

—·—

CYBERBULLYING

___/___/_____

"The words of the reckless pierce like swords, but the tongue of the wise brings healing."

- PROVERBS 12:18

C yberbullying is a very real issue that can have severe consequences. It's important to remember that the words we say online can hurt just as much as those we say in person. Imagine if someone spoke to you in the same way that you sometimes speak to others online. How would it make you feel? Remember to always treat others with kindness and respect, even when you disagree with them. If you witness cyberbullying, it's important to speak up and do what you can to help the victim.

Reflection:

Reflect on the words you use online. Are they encouraging, respectful, and uplifting to others, or do they tear others down? Make a commitment to speak with kindness and respect online.

Prayer:

Dear God,

Help me to use technology in a way that honors you and respects others. Guide me to be a positive influence and to stand up against cyberbullying.

Amen.

103

— · —

BE MINDFUL OF YOUR ONLINE PRESENCE

___/___/_____

"Whoever guards his mouth preserves his life; he who opens wide his lips comes to ruin."

- PROVERBS 13:3

I n today's digital age, it's easy to forget that what we post online can have a real impact on others and ourselves. We might think that online interactions are less important than face-to-face conversations, but that's simply not true. Every word we type and image we share has the power to build up or tear down someone else. That's why it's important to be mindful of our online presence. Before we post something, we should ask ourselves if it's something we would want to be associated with for the rest of our lives. If the answer is no, then we should think twice before hitting the "post" button. Remember, our online presence is a reflection of who we are as individuals, and we want to make sure we're presenting our best selves to the world.

Reflection:

The internet is a public space, and everything you post online can be seen by others. Spend some time reflecting on how you present yourself online, and consider the impact that your online presence may have on others. Is it a positive or negative reflection of who you are?

Prayer:

Dear God,

Guide me to use my online presence in a way that honors you and shows love and respect for others. Help me to use my words and actions to build up those around me, rather than tearing them down.

Amen.

104

— • —

HONOR YOUR PARENTS

___/___/_____

"Honor your father and your mother, so that you may live long in the land the Lord your God is giving you."

- EXODUS 20:12

The Bible teaches us to honor our parents, not just obey them. This means showing them respect, gratitude, and appreciation for all they do for us. It also means acknowledging their authority and making wise choices that honor them.

Reflection:

In what ways can you honor and respect your parents, even when you disagree with them?

Have you ever dishonored your parents? What will you do next time?

Prayer:

Dear God,

Help me to honor my parents and show them the respect they deserve. Give me the wisdom to obey them and the courage to speak truthfully with them. Amen.

105

_ . _

RESPECT YOUR SIBLINGS

___/___/_____

"Do nothing out of selfish ambition or vain conceit. Rather, in humility, value others above yourselves."

- PHILIPPIANS 2:3

Siblings are precious gifts from God, and we should treat them with love, respect, and kindness. This means being patient with them, listening to them, and helping them when they need it. It also means avoiding jealousy and competition, and seeking to build each other up.

Reflection:

Do you respect your siblings? How can you show love and respect to your siblings, even in difficult situations?

Prayer:

Dear God,

Help me to see my siblings through your eyes and to love them as you do. Teach me to be patient and understanding with them, even when it's hard.

Amen.

106

—.—

BE A PEACEMAKER

___/___/_____

"Blessed are the peacemakers, for they will be called children of God."

- MATTHEW 5:9

As Christians, we are called to be peacemakers in a world full of conflict and division. This means seeking to resolve conflicts in a peaceful and respectful way, avoiding gossip and slander, and promoting unity and harmony.

Reflection:

Have you ever had to be a peacemaker? What did you do?

How can you be a peacemaker in your daily interactions with others?

Prayer:

Dear God,

Help me to be a peacemaker in my relationships and interactions with others. Give me the wisdom and humility to resolve conflicts and promote harmony. Help me to reflect your love and peace in all that I do.

Amen.

107

FAMILY RESPONSIBILITIES

___/___/_____

"Each of you should use whatever gift you have received to serve others, as faithful stewards of God's grace in its various forms."

- I PETER 4:10

G od has given us each a role to play in our families, whether as a parent, sibling, or child. We should take these responsibilities seriously and seek to serve our family members with love and selflessness.

Reflection:

What is your role within your family?

Is there anything you can do to be better for your family?

How will you do this?

Prayer:

Dear God,

Help me to see the importance of taking responsibility for my family. Give me the strength to serve and care for them in meaningful ways. May I be a positive influence in my home and honor you through my actions.

Amen.

108

—·—

LOVE YOUR FAMILY

___/___/_____

"Love one another with brotherly affection. Outdo one another in showing honor."

- ROMANS 12:10

A bove all, we are called to love our family members as God loves us. This means showing them patience, kindness, forgiveness, and grace. It also means putting their needs before our own and seeking to build strong and healthy relationships that honor God.

Reflection:

Reflect on the time you spent with your family today. Did you show love and appreciation to your family members? How? If you didn't, what could you do next time to show it?

Prayer:

Dear God,

Please help us to love our family members unconditionally, just as you love us. Help us to be patient, forgiving, and kind towards them, and to show our love and appreciation for them in our actions and words. Guide us to be a source of support and encouragement for our family, and help us to cherish the special bond that we share.

Amen.

109

— . —

COMMUNICATION

___/___/_____

"Do not let any unwholesome talk come out of your mouths, but only what is helpful for building others up according to their needs, that it may benefit those who listen."

- EPHESIANS 4:29

Communication is not just about what we say, but how we say it. The words we speak can either tear others down or build them up. As a teen boy, it's important to remember that the way we communicate can have a big impact on those around us. Instead of using hurtful words, let's use our words to encourage and uplift others.

Reflection:

Reflect on how you communicated with others today. Did you listen actively and respond thoughtfully, or did you interrupt or speak without thinking?

Take a moment to think about how your words and actions affected those around you.

Prayer:

Dear God,

Guide me with your wisdom and grace so I can communicate effectively in the future.

Amen.

110

— · —

GIVING

___/___/_____

"But if anyone does not provide for his relatives, and especially for members of his household, he has denied the faith and is worse than an unbeliever."

- 1 Timothy 5:8

B eing giving is a valuable trait that can positively impact both the giver and the receiver. It's not just about giving money or material possessions, but also giving our time, talents, and love to others. By being generous, we can show God's love to those around us and make a difference in their lives. Whether it's volunteering at a local charity, donating to a cause we believe in, or simply being kind and helpful to others, every act of giving counts.

Reflection:

Think back over the last couple of weeks - Were there any times when you showed giving?

Were there times you could've but didn't? If so, how will you act next time?

Prayer:

Dear God,

Please help us to be generous and cheerful givers, freely sharing what we have with those in need. Help us to see opportunities to give and bless others and to do so joyfully, just as you have generously given to us.

Amen.

111

— · —

FAMILY VALUES

___/___/_____

"But as for me and my household, we will serve the Lord."

- JOSHUA 24:15

Family values are important principles and beliefs that shape the way we live our lives and interact with others. It's about putting God first in our lives and making Him the foundation of our families. By honoring our parents, being respectful to our siblings, and fulfilling our family responsibilities, we can show our love and commitment to our family. We should also strive to pass on these values to the next generation, so they, too, can live a life of purpose and meaning.

Reflection:

What are some ways that we can honor and prioritize our family values in our daily lives?

Prayer:

Dear God,

We thank you for the gift of family and for the values that guide us in our relationships with one another. Help us to live out these values in our daily lives, and to always remember the importance of cherishing and nurturing our family relationships.

Amen.

112

— · —

RACISM

___/___/_____

"There is neither Jew nor Gentile, neither slave nor free, nor is there male and female, for you are all one in Christ Jesus"

- GALATIANS 3:28

The Bible teaches that in Christ, we are all equal, regardless of race or social status. Racism has no place in the kingdom of God. As followers of Christ, we are called to love and respect all people, regardless of their race, ethnicity, or gender.

As teen boys, we have a responsibility to stand up against racism whenever we see it and treat everyone with the same respect and dignity.

Reflection:

How can we make this world more loving for all?

If you see or hear an act of racism, what will you do?

Prayer:

Dear God,

Help us to see each other through your eyes and recognize the worth of every person. Give us the strength and courage to stand up against racism and work towards building a loving world.

Amen.

113

— • —

IDENTITY IN CHRIST

___/___/_____

"So in Christ Jesus, you are all children of God through faith"

- GALATIANS 3:26

As a teen boy, you may struggle with questions about who you are and where you belong. But in Christ, you are a child of God and have a secure identity. Remember that you are loved, valued, and have a purpose in life because of your faith in Jesus. Embrace your identity in Christ and let it guide your decisions and actions every day.

Reflection:

How did your identity in Christ guide your decisions and actions today?

Prayer:

Dear God,

Help us to fully grasp our identity in Christ and to live each day with confidence and purpose rooted in our faith.

Amen.

LEAVE A REVIEW

Thanks for purchasing and reading this book. If you enjoyed it, please leave a review so I can continue to create books like this for you!

As a self-publisher, reviews and spreading the book by word-of-mouth keep the business going.

To leave a review, scan the QR code below, and you will be taken straight to the page.

Or, you can go onto the product page on Amazon (search for the book title in the search menu while on the site), scroll down to the review section to find something as you see below, and click 'Write a customer review.'

Thank you so much & God bless you. I hope to see you in the next book :)!

P.S. You can find my *other books* on my Amazon page – under the name 'Biblical Teachings'.

You can also find my group on Facebook for more devotions and early access to new releases. Scan the QR code on the next page to be taken straight to the group. Can't wait to see you there!